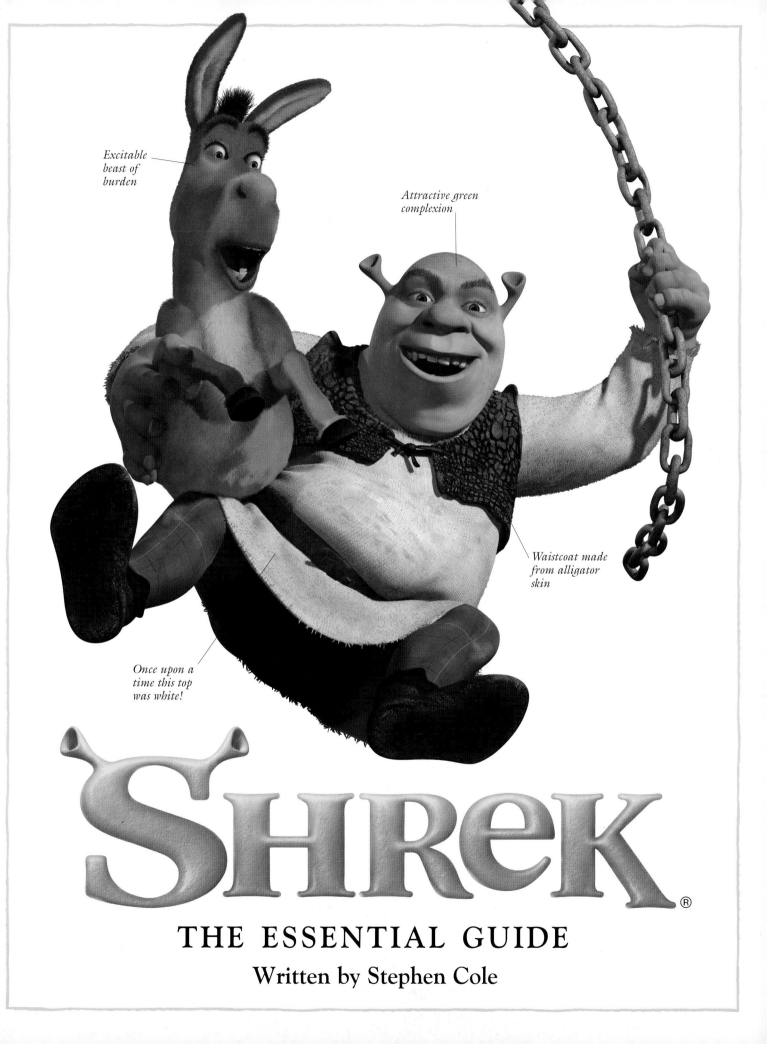

Excitable beast of burden

Attractive green complexion

Waistcoat made from alligator skin

Once upon a time this top was white!

SHREK®

THE ESSENTIAL GUIDE

Written by Stephen Cole

Contents

 **nce upon a time...**

There was a large green ogre who became a great hero... a small donkey who became his noble steed... and a beautiful princess who kept a mysterious secret.

This is their story...

Publisher's note: Please do not use pages from this book as toilet paper. This may impair your enjoyment of the tale.

Shrek

At first glance, Shrek might appear to be a big, green, terrifying ogre. At second glance, – if you've stuck around long enough for a second glance – you'd probably think much the same thing! But there's much more to Shrek than meets the eye. He may look scary, but really he's a kind ogre with a very big heart.

Resourceful ogres use their vast quantities of ear wax to make candles.

Alligator-skin waistcoat

Ogre theory

Shrek once told Donkey that ogres are like onions. No, not because they smell strongly or make you cry, but because they have *layers*. If people would only look beyond first appearances and give ogres a chance, they'd see that they're not so scary after all!

Tartan trousers – Shrek comes from a very old family of McOgres.

Extra-large leather shoes made to withstand Shrek's rancid feet

Ogres are very proud of their huge yellow teeth. Shrek uses special beetle-juice toothpaste and a gristly bone as a toothbrush to make sure his teeth are stained and his breath stays really stale!

To keep his clothes damp and covered in mildew, Shrek soaks them in stagnant swamp water and then leaves them in the shade to fester.

Cash for Creatures!

Shrek learns that a reward has been offered for the capture of any fairy tale creatures in the area. Ogres command a good price, and he is soon targeted by men eager for the booty. Luckily, a few threats and a slobbering ogre roar are enough to send even the bravest man packing!

A guard tries to arrest Shrek but soon realises he's made a big mistake!

Fight for your rights!

Hundreds of foolish knaves have tried to slay Shrek. They usually turn tail as soon as he snuffs out their flaming torches with his bare fingers! Shrek has a large collection of rakes, pitchforks, swords, and spears that they drop as they run away.

Boiled giant slug

Pumpkin stuffed with worms

Slimy eyeballs

Fish-eye tartare with squashed bugs

Dead skin flakes for seasoning

Shrek's favourite foods

Shrek's appetite is bad news for swamp life!

• He catches weedrats and roasts them over an open fire! They're also very good in stews.

• Wart-covered swamp toads are another favourite – they're especially nice in soup!

• If Shrek gets peckish after his meal, he likes to snack on eyeballs on toast – scrumptious!

Shrek's Home

A crooked, wooden shack built into a rotten old tree stump in the middle of a festering swamp – there's no place like home! The swamp is smelly, damp, and most of all, deserted – absolutely perfect for an ogre. Shrek's put up lots of KEEP OUT signs around his swamp because he likes living all alone. At least, that's what he keeps telling himself...

Ogres tend to build homes in the middle of nowhere. That's because they get bored by the sound of people screaming in fright when they walk by!

Path to Shrek's garden where he likes to grow weeds

Wipe muddy feet here – and make them muddier!

Dinner for one

Shrek may live alone but he dines in style. He lights an earwax candle and sets the table with his cutlery. One of Shrek's favourite meals is a fish supper since catching the fish is so easy! He wades into the swamp pond, lets off some truly revolting gas, and collects the dead fish when they float up to the surface!

Barrel of home-brewed ogre ale

Firewood gathered by smashing up tree-trunks

All ogre cooking is done over an open fire.

Shrek likes nothing better than a slimy mud shower to wake him up in the morning. All that gloopy muck is great as a mouthwash as well!

Water trough (also good for bathing feet)

Antique rottenwood dining table

Window for checking no one comes near

Reinforced chair to hold Shrek's weight

Far-out(side) toilet

Ogres keep their toilets outside for a good reason. The build-up of smelly ogre gases *indoors* could pose a serious health risk! Since swamps smell so bad anyway, no one really notices the extra stink outside…

For toilet paper, Shrek rips out pages from a silly old fairy tale book. He never dreams that fairy tale magic will one day touch *his* life for real!

The toilet's rickety construction is good for ventilation.

Tree house!

Living in the stump of an old tree has lots to recommend it. The roots are incredibly strong, so the house has good foundations, and the thick turf roof helps to keep the house cool in summer and warm in winter. No wonder ogres like Shrek opt for a stump every time!

Donkey

Some cultures revere the donkey as the wisest of animals. Not in this fairy tale! So when this hip-talking, fast-walking, lucky, plucky donkey charges straight into Shrek, the ogre knows that he's bound to be a gigantic pain – in more ways than one!

For all their differences, Shrek and Donkey soon become firm friends who are there for each other – no matter what.

Long ears droop when sad and perk up when happy.

Who could resist such soulful brown eyes?

High-flying Donkey

Tiring of his stubborn nature and endless chatter, Donkey's lady owner plans to hand him in for a ten-shilling reward as part of the 'cash for creatures' scheme. But luckily some fairy dust spills on Donkey, enabling him to fly away... all of three metres! To escape the guards he has to rely on his short-but-swift legs – and runs right into Shrek!

Sharing trouble

Donkey may think of himself as a brave and noble steed, but to Shrek, he's a mangy barnyard animal! Shrek has to admit, though, Donkey is very useful in a fight – his strong hind legs make him a great sidekick!

Red hot love!

This smooth-talking donkey doesn't care about looks. In fact, he sometimes gets carried away – not just by romance, but by his enormous fire-breathing dragon girlfriend!

Annoying!

• Donkey's ability to talk often surprises the people he meets. But as Shrek puts it, 'It's getting him to shut up that's the trick!'

• He's prone to blind panic – about the only thing that doesn't scare him stupid is Shrek!

• He loves to sing, wail, and whistle – but Shrek only lets him hum.

Fiona the Fair

Fiona spends her long days waiting at her window in the highest room of her tower, dreaming of the day she'll meet her true love.

After falling victim to a mysterious magical enchantment as a small girl, the beautiful Princess Fiona was sent by her parents to a far-off tower to await rescue by a handsome prince. It's a situation straight out of a fairy tale, but Fiona is not your traditional helpless heroine. Strong-willed, feisty, and smart, Fiona is a princess who really packs a punch!

An unorthodox rescue

Fiona expected to be rescued by her prince charming. Instead, she got an enormous green ogre who breaks all the rules! Rather than waking her with a gentle kiss, he shakes her by the shoulders. And when she offers him her delicate hanky as a token of gratitude to treasure, he wipes his sooty face with it!

The Princess Diaries

As a child, Fiona kept a diary full of her dreams of fairy tale happiness. Since then she's learned one or two home truths...

• A good man is hard to find – especially when he's been burnt to a crisp by a dragon while trying to rescue you!

• Perfect people are often perfectly boring!

• Looks aren't everything – and even ogres can be 'charming' in their own way!

Ponytail doubles as wicked weapon in martial arts combat!

Birds beware!

Like all good fairy tale princesses, Fiona loves birds and animals and is gifted with an incredible singing voice. But while she may have perfect pitch, there's an *im*perfect hitch – she hits notes so high they make unwary birds explode if they're perched nearby!

Royal dress designed with high kicks in mind.

Monsieur Hood

On the way to Duloc, Fiona finds herself 'rescued' from Shrek by Monsieur Hood, a silly show-off in tights! But Fiona's no drippy damsel – and Monsieur Hood and his merry men are the ones in distress by the time the high-kicking princess has taught them a lesson!

Flat slippers – more practical than Cinderella's glass ones

Fairy Tale Squatters

No more 'gnome sweet gnome' for this elf.

Shrek gets quite a shock when he discovers hundreds of fairy tale characters camping out in his swamp! Lord Farquaad, fed up with magical folk lowering the tone of his perfect kingdom, has had them all chucked out. With no place to go, the fairy tale folk pack up their troubles – and dump them right at Shrek's door!

Character Key

1 Grand Wizard

2 Straw House Pig

3 Tom Thumb

4 Shoemaker's Elf

5 Leprechaun

6 Children of the Shoe

7 Trainee Wizard

8 Bashful Dwarf

9 Happy Dwarf

10 Brick & Stick Pigs

Witches and wizards don't usually mix – they always argue over whose hat is pointiest.

Shrek likes his privacy – he doesn't want squatters on his land!

Birds of a feather

The fairy tale characters band together in their time of crisis. Wicked witches co-exist peacefully with good elves, The Old Lady Who Lived In A Shoe takes on lodgers at very reasonable rates, and the Pied Piper generously donates some rats to be roasted over the campfires.

The Old Lady made the most of her shoe-space by adding an attractive loft conversion.

After a lifetime of 'happy ever afters', the fairy tale characters have no idea what to do when they lose their homes. They need a hero… and Shrek might just fit the bill!

A number of homeless witches are guided down to Shrek's swamp by beacons like this campfire.

6

Fairy tale folk insist on clean laundry, even in a crisis.

7

5

3

4

9

8

Donkey was resigned to a lonely night spent outside Shrek's house – he didn't expect this much company!

Pinocchio keeps busy by trying to convince people he's a real boy.

Happy Ever After?

A bunch of dwarves used to dwell in Duloc. Then the townspeople rounded them up and handed them over to Farquaad's guards in exchange for gold.

Elves, unicorns, fairies, witches, a whole truckload of talking animals... it looks like there'll be no fairy tale ending for these magical characters, forced by Farquaad to live in Shrek's swamp! The grumpy ogre doesn't want them on his land, and sets out to have them removed. But once his adventures have softened his heart just a little, Shrek realises that fairy tale company can actually be fun – and he lets them visit whenever they like!

Three Little Pigs

These Bavarian pigs are light on their trotters, and love to dance up a storm! They were happily living as bachelor pigs in traditional houses of straw, sticks, and bricks before Lord Farquaad came along. He huffed and he puffed and... signed an eviction notice, leaving the Three Little Pigs homeless!

Fascinating fairy tale facts

• The three blind mice carry 'stunt' tails so the farmer's wife can cut them off without mess or injury.

• The big bad wolf wears old ladies' clothes even when he's *not* trying to eat Red Riding Hood.

• The three little pigs stay on strict diets to make sure they *remain* little.

Gordo, bravest of the blind mice, chomps on Shrek's ear thinking it is cheese. His verdict? 'Filthy stuff!'

The Big Bad Wolf

An old-fashioned wolf, he sticks to the tricks he knows: dress up like an old woman and blow down pigs' houses before they master the art of cement-mixing. Everyone's wise to his tricks, but the wolf doesn't care – he prefers to take it easy all day in other people's beds!

When The Three Bears are evicted from their home they worry about who'll be sitting in their chairs, eating their porridge, and sleeping in their beds!

This pig sticks with a house made of twigs. He's no stranger to homelessness.

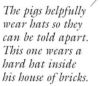

Grandma's nightdress

The pigs helpfully wear hats so they can be told apart. This one wears a hard hat inside his house of bricks.

Losing his flimsy home is never the final straw for this little pig.

17

Boy and Man

Pinocchio and the Gingerbread
Man are two fairy tale characters
thrown together by fate, destined to
become good friends both to each other
and to Shrek. When Shrek leaves his
beloved swamp to visit the Kingdom of
Far Far Away, Gingy and Pinocchio
help housesit. And when they
learn he's in trouble, the pair
lead the charge to save him –
in unique style!

Pinocchio hopes to be a real
boy one day.

I wooden lie!

To Pinocchio, honesty is very important
– if he tells a fib, his nose grows as long
as a flagpole! When the old man who
carved him decides to hand him over for
a reward, Pinocchio tries to convince the
guard captain he's a real boy. But his
nose betrays him, and Pinocchio is
locked up for being a 'possessed toy'!

*Wooden head
(no puppet
strings
attached)*

*Nose extends
dramatically
whenever
Pinocchio lies.*

*The captain offers
only five shillings
for Pinocchio.*

*Pinocchio's
carver takes
it gladly.*

*Large carved feet
to weigh down
body*

18

Tough cookie

The Gingerbread Man may look soft and sweet, but in fact he is one tough cookie! When kidnapped and tortured by Lord Farquaad, he bravely refuses to reveal the whereabouts of Duloc's remaining fairy tale creatures.

Soft icing features

Special gumdrop buttons

He's wholesome and true – just what you'd expect from a biscuit made from organic flour.

When the chocolate chips are down, Gingy stays steadfast and loyal. He's a courageous cookie who never gives up!

He's ginger-bred!

• He is a super-fast runner – as the rhyme goes, 'You can't catch me, I'm the Gingerbread Man!'

• Should one of his biscuity legs snap off, he simply uses a candy cane crutch till he can get patched up!

• He is a close personal friend of the Muffin Man, who lives on Drury Lane.

• The possessions he prizes most are his gumdrop buttons – both fashionable and delicious!

Gingerbread mansion

Gingy owns a spectacular holiday home in a magical forest outside of Duloc – one that's good enough to eat! Working from Hansel and Gretel's eye-witness accounts of a similar edible property, the Gingerbread handy man has built a munchable mansion with stunning views of the marzipan surroundings.

After a little accident, Gingy loses his soft icing features – but he finds them eventually!

Lord Farquaad

Scheming expression

A wicked little man with big ambitions, Lord Farquaad is obsessed with perfection. He's banished all fairy tale creatures from the kingdom of Duloc, since they don't fit in with his vision of a perfect world.
Despite his big chin, page boy hairdo, and vertically-challenged physique, Farquaad thinks he'll make the perfect king – and desires the perfect bride!

Manly frame (with a little help from padded shoulders)

Adjustable table can be lowered and raised according to height of torturer.

Cookie cruelty

Determined to rid himself of every last fairy tale creature, Farquaad cruelly tortures the Gingerbread Man to find where they're hiding. He's even prepared to remove Gingy's treasured gumdrop buttons!

Swishing cape for dramatic exits

Farquaad's castle is the biggest bachelor pad ever built – for the smallest occupant! Each night he combs his body hair and dreams of his perfect bride...

Farquaad's blind date

Lord Farquaad wants to be king, but the Magic Mirror points out that first he must marry a princess. Currently available are house-maid blonde, Cinderella; slumbering brunette Snow White; and a fiery redhead from a dragon-guarded castle – Fiona! For Farquaad there's no competition… Fiona is his perfect pick!

The Magic Mirror has dealt with many vain tyrants, but Farquaad really takes the cake – (so long as he can reach the table it's on, that is!)

Fun with Thelonius!

Thelonius is Farquaad's head henchman. Here are his magical tips for tip-top torture!

• Intimidate at all times. If your Magic Mirror gets lippy, scare him into silence by smashing a similar shiny object.

• Don't be squeamish. If that Gingerbread Man won't talk – dunk him in milk!

• Don't mix business with pleasure – it's bad manners to eat someone you've just tortured.

Under that hood, he might be quite a good-looking guy.

Choosing a champion

Freeing Fiona is a dangerous mission. Farquaad offers Shrek his swamp back if he agrees to rescue her. Of course, Shrek may die while trying, but that's a sacrifice Lord Farquaad is willing to make!

Even after he's met his doom, Farquaad's vanity lives on. A massive gravestone is erected, showing him in heroic battle against an enormous dragon. As if!

Duloc

At the edge of a giant cornfield stands the city of Duloc – the fortress home of Lord Farquaad. Like the man himself, it's insanely neat and orderly. The trees are clipped into perfect cones... the buildings are smart and spotless... cheery music is piped through speakers... souvenir booths are filled with figurines of Lord Farquaad... In fact, it's just like living in a theme park – but without any of the fun rides!

Residents of Duloc always form orderly lines with the help of ropes and bollards... but ogres don't believe in queueing!

Every stone that went into Farquaad's castle was individually selected by the builders to make sure that the entire building is flawless. They didn't fancy a spell in the dungeon!

One of Farquaad's perfect penthouses

The castle

Lord Farquaad's castle towers high above every other building in Duloc – it's a massive home for such a minute man! The under-sized ruler loves to gaze out over his perfect kingdom from one of his luxury penthouses – there's not a finer view for miles around. But Lord Farquaad loves his bedchamber best of all. With its big round bed and snuggly zebra-print sheets, he's guaranteed a perfect night's sleep!

High stone walls surround the entire kingdom to keep out any riff-raff who might lower the tone!

The dungeons are justly famous as the most hygienic in the land.

Duloc Cathedral has a huge stained-glass window... of Lord Farquaad.

Beautiful buildings

You'll find that all the buildings in Duloc are kept spotlessly clean. That's because armed guards helpfully remind the peasants to wash them carefully each hour, on the hour! And don't miss the beautiful gardens – each blade of grass is snipped by hand!

Turnstile trauma

Just like the theme park it resembles, to get into Duloc you have to walk through the turnstiles. But if you've got four legs, that's not so easy! Donkey somehow squeezes his whole body inside the turnstile – which spins him around and spits him out on the ground!

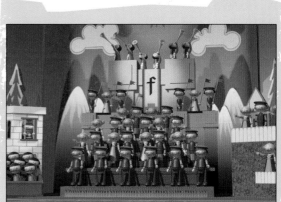

The rules of Duloc

All visitors to Duloc are met with this single scintillating song...

Welcome to Duloc, such a perfect town
Here we have some rules
Let us lay them down
Don't make waves, stay in line
And we'll get along fine!
Please keep off the grass
Shine your shoes, wipe your... face
Duloc is... Duloc is...
DULOC IS A
PERFECT PLACE!

Gone Questing

At first, the journey from Duloc to the castle where Fiona resides is quite pleasant on the eyes, all sunflower fields and lush forests... It's less pleasant on the ears, though, at least for Shrek – he has to listen to Donkey's endless chattering! Then, as they draw closer to Fiona's lonely castle prison, the greenery turns brown, the grass stops growing... and all is barren, blackened, and burnt!

There's an awful smell as Shrek and Donkey approach their destination... But for once the odour is not caused by Shrek – it's actually brimstone from the local volcano!

Hot-footing it!

It's not only the lava moat surrounding the castle that's hot stuff – so is the dragon who guards it! Shrek barely manages to save Donkey and the princess without being fried!

With Donkey seconds from plunging into a sea of boiling lava, Shrek lends a hand and grabs a leg.

Rottenwood bridge is extremely flammable

A Lava-ly view

The rickety rope bridge that leads to the castle is scary at the best of times. But when you're trying to cross it with an angry dragon right behind you it gets a whole lot scarier! Dragon turns half of it to ashes with a huge fireball... but Shrek, Donkey, and Fiona cling on to the other half and climb it like a rope ladder. Phew!

Castles – HOT Property!

Have YOU ever thought about owning a castle?

• Got younger brothers or sisters? Dragon-guarded castles offer an excellent alternative to nurseries.

• Castles with their own fire-breathing dragons and volcanoes benefit from low heating costs.

• No more noisy neighbours.

• Castles are cool! Especially in winter (brrrr!).

Dragon has her own private chamber in the bowels of the castle. To make it pretty she has filled it with piles of dragon treasure!

GNOME SWEET GNOME ESTATE AGENTS

This stylishly dilapidated, sinister castle is conveniently located on a crumbling pinnacle of rock in a sea of molten lava, just three days' quest from the nearest shops. Would suit hermit or princess suffering wicked enchantment. Viewing highly recommended

Dragon

Charged with guarding Princess Fiona within her castle prison, Dragon lives as lonely a life as the princess herself. While she has slain many valiant knights who have hoped to release Fiona from captivity with her searing fire, deep down, Dragon is tender-hearted, and only wants to be loved!

Dragon's wings are powerful.

Dragon never forgets to put on her lipstick – you never know when the donkey of your dreams might appear!

You're fired!

With so few visitors coming to call – and since those that do are all boring old knights come to do battle with her – it's no wonder that Dragon gets kind of crabby. Convinced that the world is out to get her, her policy is to incinerate visitors first and ask questions later – that's until a small, nervous donkey melts her heart!

Powerful throwing arms make the winter knights fly by.

Huge clawed feet for squashing the strongest armour

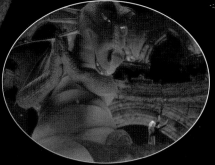

When Donkey is caught by Dragon he tries to flatter his way out of trouble! The scaly lady takes his compliments to heart – and loses her heart to him!

Dragon's love tips

• Line your lair with gold and gemstones – they set off the gleam in your eyes!

• Keep your teeth white and sparkly by flossing regularly!

• There's nothing like lighting a gothic candelabra with your fiery breath to create a romantic atmosphere for you and your beast of burden!

Giant, whip-like tail can smash through solid stone.

Set free... to do what?

Once Fiona has been rescued from the castle, Dragon has no one to watch over. She gets very depressed. Donkey meets her again after falling out with Shrek – and the two ease their loneliness by staying together.

A royal pardon-me!

Donkey and Dragon both believe in making a dramatic entrance – so when Fiona needs rescuing from Lord Farquaad's clutches, the pair dive through Duloc Cathedral's finest stained glass window! As an encore, Dragon swallows Farquaad whole – but burps back up his crown!

Strange Enchantment

By night one way, by day another,
This shall be the norm.
Until you find true love's first kiss
And then take love's true form.

This terrible curse was put on Fiona when she was just a little girl. While she is fair and beautiful by day, when the sun sets she becomes a green ogress! Her parents sent her away so that a prince might some day rescue her, fall in love, and kiss her to break the spell.

The trouble with true love is that it can be unpredictable. It's like eating weedrat – who would have thought that something so gross could taste so good? And who would ever think that a big ogre could be so truly lovely? Why... Fiona would!

Putting his hoof in it!

Donkey's choice of words when he first sees the ogress Fiona is a little unfortunate...

• 'Oh my God, you ate the princess!'

• 'I *told* Shrek those rats were a bad idea!'

• 'You're not that ugly...Well, OK, I'm not going to lie. You ARE ugly...!'

Donkey is not famed for his silver tongue.

Can't face the face

Fiona hates the way she looks at night – she thinks she's a horrible, ugly beast. That's why she plans to marry Lord Farquaad quickly, hoping he can break the spell before he discovers her secret.

Something... green?

There's an old wedding tradition that brides should wear something old, something new, something borrowed, something blue. But Fiona's already blue because she's green at night – and it's Shrek that she really wants to marry!

When Shrek kisses Fiona and breaks the spell, she takes true love's form at last... the form of an ogress! Shrek is delighted; someone who really loves you always sees your true beauty!

Ogress Fiona

There are many clues to Princess Fiona's secret ogress side: she enjoys a hearty belch as much as Shrek does; she can inflate a snake with ease and make a great balloon sculpture out of it; she possesses all the fearsome fighting skills of a furious ogress; and her heart is so big it could only beat inside a true ogress!

Fiona's ears now stick out through her hair.

Dress made from stretchy material to allow for Fiona's transformations

DAILY
ROYAL WEDD

It was a right royal disaster for Lord Farquaad today when he accidentally married an OGRESS and then got eaten by a DRAGON!

In front of a large crowd of admiring well-wishers (the penalty for non-attendance was death), Lord Farquaad believed he was about to marry the beautiful Princess Fiona – but this was far from a perfect wedding!

Things started to go wrong when notorious ogre SHREK burst into the cathedral objecting to the marriage. But they soon grew worse for Farquaad as his new bride turned into a GREEN ogress, much to the startled Shrek's delight.

The new king tried to banish both ogres, but was interrupted by a giant dragon crashing through the stained-glass window and swallowing him up in one gulp.

DULOC

1 New Penny

NG SHOCKER

THE DRAGON'S DRIVER, Donkey, observed, 'Celebrity marriages – they never last do they?' Fiona is soon to marry again – to Shrek. It is believed they will be living happily ever after.

Just Married

Donkey was hoping that the quest he shared with Shrek would have a happy ending – and it certainly did! With Lord Farquaad out of the way, Shrek and Fiona got married in the swamp. They invited everyone in Duloc and had an amazing party before setting off on a honeymoon neither of them would ever forget!

Contented smile

Love blossoms

A party in a swamp may not be everyone's idea of a dream wedding, but for ogres it's the perfect choice! Shrek remembered Donkey's advice on romance, and had the whole swamp festooned with fabulous flowers.

A fairy turned an onion into a fine wedding carriage and turned the three blind mice into white chargers and a driver!

Honeymoon and beyond!

Fiona and Shrek have a wonderful honeymoon – they frolic in the sea, stay in a gingerbread house, taunt fearful villagers and spend long warm nights in a hot tub of mud! But on their return home, the newlyweds are invited to visit the Kingdom of Far Far Away, where Fiona's parents – the King and Queen – wish to hold a royal ball in honour of her marriage. Donkey insists on coming along too, since he's already missed out on all the honeymoon fun!

Traditional ogre swimsuit

Donkey set for fun!

Far Far Away, as its name suggests, is… far, far away! Shrek, Fiona and Donkey travel over mountains and bridges, through field and vale… and through about 20 different time zones!

Carriage fever

Shrek's nervous on the trip to Far Far Away. He is worried that the King and Queen will never accept an ogre as their son-in-law. To make matters worse, Donkey soon gets bored by the long journey. He plays I Spy, keeps asking 'Are we there yet?' and makes lots of annoying POP noises!

Long, difficult journeys are not made easier by hyperactive donkeys.

Far Far Away

Some say that Hollywood is the place where fairy tales can come true... but in a kingdom where fairy tales are real, Far Far Away is the place where dreams can come true! All the fairy tale princes and princesses flock here to live happily ever after in luxury, making the most of their well-earned celebrity status.

Far Far Away is an exotic land of champagne wishes and caviar dreams. Fiona was sent to a dragon-guarded tower when she was just a girl, so she's really excited to be back!

Adoring crowds

Fiona's homecoming is a big deal in Far Far Away – the crowds are out in force to celebrate the long-awaited return of the beautiful Princess Fiona and her new husband! But cheers turn to gasps of horror as Fiona and Shrek step from their onion carriage with Donkey...

Fiona gets the red carpet treatment.

Things can get hairy at Rapunzel's pad!

Who lives where?

• Rapunzel has her own luxurious split-level turret where she plays with her hair all day long.

• Snow White is now waited upon in a magnificent mansion by 700 dwarves. She has removed all apple trees from the grounds.

• Beauty has her own glittering palace, while Beast enjoys a spacious kennel in the garden.

• Goldilocks has found a house that's just right!

It's said the streets of Far Far Away are paved with gold… This is not strictly true; they're actually a mix of cobblestones and concrete.

Wearing a brave face

Face-to-face with his parents-in-law at last, Shrek forces a smile. 'It's easy to see where Fiona gets her good looks from,' he says… but they are NOT amused!

Heads of State

F iona's parents – King Harold and Queen Lillian – are rulers of the Kingdom of Far Far Away. When they locked their daughter away in a tower, they always assumed a handsome prince would come to her rescue. Now, after many years, they are surprised when their beautiful daughter turns up, not only in the company of an ogre – but looking like one too!

The King and Queen live in a modest little palace with just 128 bedrooms and three dozen twinkling turrets.

Regal crown set with sapphires

King Harold

The King is shocked that Fiona has chosen to marry an ogre, and makes no secret of his dislike for Shrek. What nobody knows is that the king made a secret deal with Fairy Godmother a long time ago and things have not gone according to plan...

The royal goatee – king of beards

Ermine trim paw-stitched by mouse tailors

Sumptuous royal robes

Dinner disaster

Harold and Lillian lay on a special dinner to welcome Shrek and Fiona, but Shrek's not used to royal manners. He slurps down the snails with their shells still on. He drinks the water from the finger bowls thinking it's soup and then accidentally swallows a spoon before coughing it back up at high speed. His ogre ways offend King Harold and upset Fiona… but at least Donkey's happy – the food's great!

King Harold disapproves of having an ogre in the family, and Shrek thinks the King has been a bad father. Can the two men in Fiona's life *ever* get along?

Queen Lillian

The Queen believes in the power of true love – and in not judging by first appearances. While Shrek is certainly no handsome prince, she tries to make the best of things since he and her daughter are clearly so happy together. Always polite and understanding, she is a wise and popular ruler.

Delicate golden crown studded with royal rubies

Far, far away look in the royal eyes at all times

Solid gold stitching

Pink gown to bring out the colour of the royal cheeks

Finest elf embroidery

Fairy Godmother

Every princess comes with a Fairy Godmother… what Fiona doesn't realise is that hers is a wicked, ambitious schemer! Always surrounded by burly bodyguards, her motto is 'Happiness is just a teardrop away…' but it's *her* happiness she's thinking of! And she wants Shrek out of the way for her own selfish reasons!

Perfectly styled hair

Prim glasses convey 'professional' image to clients.

Delicate magic wand for casting sensitive spells

Flinty fairy

According to this Fairy Godmother, Ogres are not allowed 'happy ever afters'. She believes that Shrek should slope off back to the swamp by himself and let her clean up the 'mess' he's made of Princess Fiona's life!

Fairy Godmother's appetite is legendary. When she tells her son she could eat him all up, she *may* not be kidding!

Fairy favourite foods

The 'abracadabra diva' always pigs out at times of stress…

• She secretly loves a trip down to Friar's Fat Boy, the medieval drive-through!

• Her favourite order is a Renaissance Wrap and chilli rings… but hold the mayo!

• Her top dessert is anything deep fried and covered in chocolate!

Gossamer fairy wings reinforced to carry great weight

Prince Charming

Highly handsome, vain, and spoilt, Prince Charming is Fairy Godmother's brattish son. He trusts his mother when she says that one day he will be king! Pity poor Far Far Away should that ever happen – his most pressing royal business will be deciding which colour hat best brings out his razzle-dazzle!

Delicate fingers for skillfully combining spell ingredients

Some hero!

Prince Charming hoped to rescue Fiona from her castle prison, but Shrek beat him to it. The prince didn't dare go in until Dragon moved out – not realising that Fiona had left too! When he found out that she had married another, he ran straight back to his mother – who vowed to fix things...

The Poison Apple

here are some places in Far Far Away that law-abiding folk should steer well clear of... and the Poison Apple pub is one of them! You'll find no airy-fairy tale characters here – only black-hearted rogues and scoundrels. If you're looking for a fight, a mug of ale in bad company, or even a villain for hire, the Poison Apple is the place to come!

The doorman at the Poison Apple is a cyclops. He keeps an eye on the people that come in!

The Ugly Stepsister

The Poison Apple's number one barmaid is Doris, one of Cinderella's ugly stepsisters. Some say she looks like a lumberjack in a dress! But be that as it may, she has a big heart and has found true love with one of her wicked regulars, Captain Hook. All the regulars at the Poison Apple value her wisdom and good advice.

Sinister forest location for added atmosphere

Bleak, unwelcoming appearance to scare off the faint-hearted

Get your rotten ale from these!

Even the king conducts business here...

If you can't grow a poison apple, drink there instead!

Someone couldn't pay his bar bill...

Paying regulars

• **Captain Hook** is the poison apple of Doris's eye. He doesn't let his *hand*icap stop him playing piano!

• If you can't see the wood for the **Trees** that drink here, ask them to move... but you'd better ask nicely!

• Many **pirates** linger here, busy swapping tall tales and treasure trails, me hearty!

• The **Headless Horseman** likes to throw a drink down his neck!

Hatching plots

There are times when you can't move in the Poison Apple for nefarious plans being hatched all around you. But it's not often a king comes to visit! The King asks the Ugly Stepsister if she knows anyone who can take care of an ogre. 'There's only one fella who can handle a job like that,' she tells him, 'and frankly, he don't like to be disturbed!' But the king is not to be put off...

Out of sight, in the darkened back room of the Poison Apple, a pair of green eyes glint at the sight of gold... a wicked deal is struck... and soon, a mysterious feline adventurer will embark on a daring new mission!

Puss In Boots

He is a fierce feline – an adventurer for hire. He's an acrobatic cat with a smooth Spanish accent, fearless and unbeatable in combat – unless he gets a furball! His name is… Puss In Boots! Offered a bag of gold in exchange for 'taking care' of Shrek, Puss confidently accepts. His encounter with Shrek doesn't quite go according to plan, and as a result the two become allies. Shrek soon learns that Puss can be a canny cat to have around!

Should his dazzling battle skills and smooth Spanish charm ever fail him, Puss has another way to get what he wants – he plays the helpless, wide-eyed kitty. Works every time!

Cold steel

The cat and the donkey

Donkey is cross when Shrek agrees to Puss sharing their adventures – he feels the feisty feline is muscling in on his job as Shrek's best friend. But once the two loyal animals stop competing for Shrek's affections, they learn that they can *both* make a first rate ogre-support team – by working together!

The Puss of myth and song

Puss In Boots has a memorable way with words… Here are just a few of his top-quality quotes!

• 'Ha! ha! Fear me… if you DARE! HISSSSS!'

• 'Now, ye ogre, pray for mercy from… Puss In Boots!'

• 'Take off the powdered wig, and step away from your drawers!'

• 'I was just concocting this very plan! Already our minds are becoming one!'

A bargain struck

After a battle in which Puss nearly loses one of his nine stylish lives, the dashing cat decides he may have misjudged the ogre. He tells Shrek, 'On my honour, I am obliged to accompany you until I have saved your life as you have spared me mine.'

Stylish black hat with primrose yellow plume

Cape for full swashbuckling effect

Special 'kitty customised' miniature rapier

Buccaneering belt

Striped tail for perfect poise and balance

Dashing leather boots (can be leapt right out of in an emergency).

Like all cats, Puss is helpless if he's grabbed by the scruff of his neck. When Shrek catches him, the powerless Puss can only beg for mercy – and the grumpy ogre lets him off lightly.

Potion Factory

In the middle of an enchanted glade stands Fairy Godmother's incredible potion factory. From the vast array of colourful ingredients that are kept here she conjures her world-famous potions… But will her 'Happily Ever After' spell work for Shrek?

To ensure even mixing, an elfin centrifuge puts ingredients in a spin!

Giant wheel helps turn a conveyor belt – potion in motion!

Catwalk for overseeing elves at work

Potions aren't made from magic alone – there's plenty of complex chemistry used too!

Liquid love

The elves can barely keep up with public demand for Fairy Godmother's love potion… there's a drop of desire and a pinch of passion in every bottle!

Ingredients are mixed together in huge vats.

Each bottle is filed alphabetically.

As a safety precaution, powerful potions are kept behind glass.

The Potion Storage Room contains thousands of potions.

Ingredients travel on rails to the vats as required.

Bad for your elf!

The potions require very careful handling and the elfin workers wear special protective suits. Security elves are employed to guard the potions from any would-be thieves.

Magical map of the kingdom helps elves to keep track of potion deliveries.

Most popular potions

Fairy Godmother's top-selling spells...

• Warm Spell Potion – guaranteed to make the coldest day sunny and bright!

• Elfa Seltzer – if you're feeling flat, a swig of this will make you as perky as a pixie!

• Oinkment – shrinks your stomach when you can't stop pigging out!

Elfa Seltzer

Warm Spell Potion

Oinkment

Transformation!

Thinking that Fiona would be happier if he was handsome and no longer an ogre, Shrek (and Donkey) drink a 'Happily Ever After' potion. Soon, the two of them are magically transformed into magnificent males. But is this *really* the look that Fiona will go for, or is Shrek making a terrible mistake?

Powdered wig

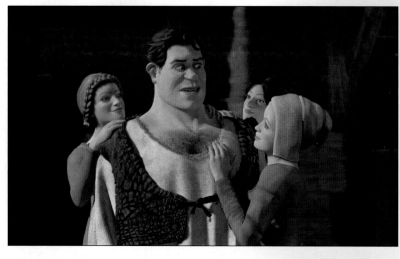

Change for the better?

Shrek finds that with his cute button nose and wavy hair, he is now irresistible to women! Donkey agrees that Shrek is now easier on the eyes, but *inside* he's still the same cranky, stanky ogre he's always been!

Much to his delight, Donkey is transformed into a magnificent stallion. He can now whinny, preen, gallop, and trot like a truly noble steed!

Puss reads that the potion may cause some alarming side-effects – including burning, itching, oozing, and weeping… UGH!

Hold up!

Since Shrek's old clothes are now far too big for him, Puss and Donkey 'find' him some new ones – they hold up some noblemen, highwayman-style, and take theirs!

Same cheeky Donkey eyes

Showdown!

Fairy Godmother plans to fool Fiona into thinking that Prince Charming is actually the new, handsome Shrek. She even brews a potion to make Fiona fall in love with him. Learning the truth, Shrek and his friends are set for a showdown with Fairy Godmother and Charming at the royal ball… but even with help from their friends, will their adventure end happily ever after?

Donkey finds he has a new talent – he can count by tapping his hoof!

Always the same…

While it may be fun to swap their old bodies for new ones, Shrek and Donkey don't really want to stay that way. It's what's inside that counts, and these two friends will always be there for each other. And that's just the way Fiona likes it!

LONDON, NEW YORK, MUNICH,
MELBOURNE, AND DELHI

ART EDITOR Guy Harvey   **PROJECT EDITOR** Lindsay Fernandes

ART DIRECTOR Mark Richards   **PUBLISHING MANAGER** Cynthia O'Neill Collins

JACKET Christopher Branfield   **CATEGORY PUBLISHER** Alex Kirkham

DTP DESIGNER Dean Scholey   **PRODUCTION** Nicola Torode

First published in Great Britain in 2004 by Dorling Kindersley Limited,
80 Strand, London, WC2R 0RL
A Penguin Company

04 05 06 07 08 10 9 8 7 6 5 4

ISBN 1-4053-0423-5

Reproduced by Media Development and Printing Ltd, UK
Printed and bound by L.E.G.O. S.p.A., Italy

Acknowledgments
DK Publishing would like to thank:
Kristy Cox, Corinne Antoniades, and the staff at DreamWorks L.L.C.;
Roger Harris for additional artworks.

Discover more at
www.dk.com

JUST
MARRIED